the *holy* SPIRIT

b a p t i s m • m i n i s t r y

P A S T O R   B O B   C O Y

The Holy Spirit
Copyright © 2008 by Calvary Chapel Church, Inc.

Requests for information should be addressed to:
Calvary Chapel Church, Inc.
Department of Communications
2401 West Cypress Creek Road
Fort Lauderdale, Florida 33309

Calvary Chapel Church website: www.Calvaryftl.org

ISBN: 1-932283-19-6

Scripture quotations marked (NKJV) are taken from the NEW KING JAMES VERSION. Copyright © 1982 by Thomas Nelson, Inc. Used by permission of Thomas Nelson. All rights reserved.

Scripture quotations marked (NLT) are from the HOLY BIBLE, NEW LIVING TRANSLATION, Copyright © 1996. Used by permission of Tyndale House Publishers, Inc., Wheaton, Illinois 60189. All rights reserved.

Compiled by Margaret DeStefano
Edited by Ana Steele
Cover and Interior Design by Deven Christopher
Project Management by The Caleb Group

Printed in the United States of America

CONTENTS

BAPTISM OF THE HOLY SPIRIT

INTRODUCTION

What happens in your head and heart when you hear the phrase, "Baptism of the Holy Spirit"? I am certain that if we polled the body of Christ, we would find quite an array of answers. Let me endeavor to reduce the response pool into three possible classifications.

The first group of people would be those who fall into a category I would term ignorant and concerned – ignorant, not in the sense of dumb or stupid, but in the sense that they just don't know much about the topic; and concerned, because what they do know gives rise to questions and even wariness. The only input they have about the Baptism of the Holy Spirit comes from a story they heard from a friend who has a relative who goes to a church where they embrace the doctrine of the Baptism of the Holy Spirit, and, to say the least, the story was just plain weird. Midway through the church service, strange things started to happen. People were rolling around on the floor and swinging from the chandeliers. Sawdust was flying everywhere. It was definitely a decisive case for concern. Now, if this is your only information or basis for belief relating to this doctrine, then it is no wonder you don't mind staying ignorant on the subject. I understand that.

The second group in the response pool is made up of those who can approach the subject with insight and confidence. They have already taken the time to study the subject, and, for this reason, they are thrilled that this book has been written. They know how important the Baptism of the Holy Spirit doctrine is for the body of Christ, and they want others to get in on it, too.

The third group includes the majority of you who have picked up this book. You are serious students of the Scripture. You open the Word, study it, divide it, and discover doctrine. You don't turn cynical or skeptical when someone mentions the Baptism of the Holy Spirit, but, on the other hand, you're not entirely confident that you have all the insight you need to understand what it means, so you're interested and even curious because you know for a fact that any biblical doctrine lived out through your own life day after day will begin to make a difference that others can see.

I pray that if you are in Category One or Category Three that the message on the pages of this book will move you into Category Two and into a position to embrace this doctrine with deeper insight and confidence so that your life may be empowered by God to draw others into His Kingdom.

Before I go much further, and for the sake of staying on

the same page with my readers, I want to clarify certain
terms that get tossed about when it comes to the Holy
Spirit. I know how it happens: you're at your workplace;
you've been going to a Bible-teaching church for a few
weeks, and then some guy at the office spots the fact that
something is slightly different about you. So he says,
"Hey, what's going on in your life?" And you say, "Well,
lately I've been going to this church." And he asks,
"What kind of church is it?" You answer, "I'm going to
that Calvary Chapel church where they teach the Bible."
Then he pops the first question, "Is that church 'Spirit-
filled'?" You are not sure exactly how to answer. "Spirit-
filled? I really don't know what you mean," you reply.
Then he uses a few more terms typically heard in
Christian circles that can be real tricky. His questions go
something like this, "Is your pastor 'charismatic' and does
he believe in 'spiritual gifts' and that they are for today?"
By now you might be thinking, "Is my pastor 'Spirit-
filled' and 'charismatic'? Well ... I don't know. Does he
believe in 'spiritual gifts'? I have no idea. And what
exactly does 'for today' mean anyway?"

Let's look at what the Bible advises about this subject.

*(1 Corinthians 12:1 NKJV) Now concerning spiritual gifts,
brethren, I do not want you to be ignorant...*

The apostle Paul cautioned the very first church that
when it came to spiritual matters, he didn't want anyone
to be ignorant. And yet, in the church today, when it
comes to spiritual matters, it seems to me that there is

"Now concerning
spiritual gifts,
brethren,
I do not want
you to be ignorant…"

1 CORINTHIANS 12:1 NKJV

way too much ignorance. We tend to fall into one of two camps. There are some churches that push the Holy Spirit aside because they are a little ignorant about spiritual matters, even though they are kind of concerned. They feel a need to understand everything that happens in their life. They want a program where they can see what is going to happen, in what order, and when. Anything that deviates from the program, regardless of how miraculous or wonderful, is not a welcomed part of their agenda. They are not prepared for anything spiritual.

It is stunting to our Christian growth when we take the heart of the Holy Spirit and push Him into this place where He has no room to function in the realm in which He exists. Remember, the Bible teaches that God is Spirit. Those who worship Him must worship Him in spirit and truth. If we are going to take the third equal part of the triune Godhead and push Him to the side because we are afraid of spiritual things, we will be left with vain religion.

There is a dynamic of the Holy Spirit that works in and through the Christian faith. We must be open to spiritual things if we are to enjoy the work of the Spirit. But be careful. If we are not in the camp of crowding out the Holy Spirit, we might dangerously fall into the opposite stance of spiritualizing everything and attributing things to God's Spirit that He would never do. You might have been to or heard of one of these types of churches. In these churches, the believer's entire relationship with God is reduced to feeling and sensing the move of the Spirit. People claim to be feeling the Holy Spirit or receiving special things from God, but, as an onlooker, you wonder what in the world is going on?

Do you see the extremes? On one side, churches approach the doctrine of the Baptism of the Holy Spirit with the attitude that they received all of the Spirit they needed at salvation. On the other side, they are so baptized in the Holy Spirit, they are drowning in a pool of senseless practices that do not bring glory to God or draw anyone nearer to the place of wanting to know Christ.

Hence, there is a problem on both sides. The problem is that neither side has taken the time to look carefully at Jesus Christ. Jesus Christ was the most Spirit-filled Man to ever have walked the earth. When we look at His life and read through the records of Matthew, Mark, Luke, and John, what do we find? First, let me tell you what we don't find. We don't find Matthew recording for us: "And then Jesus, filled with the Spirit, began to shake violently; then He began to bark like a dog; and then He began to roll around on the floor like a wild animal. He was filled with the Spirit." No, every time Jesus was filled with the Spirit, He did something that made us look on and admire Him, respect Him, and want to be just like Him. Why is it, then, that sometimes when I turn on Christian television, those "filled with the Holy Spirit" cause me to say, "What is that? I don't remember ever seeing Jesus behave like that. I don't know of a time in the Bible that I remember them doing that. What's going on here?"

Let me say, as tactfully and lovingly as I can, sometimes those "works" of the Spirit are nothing more than manifestations of the flesh. Our flesh loves attention. I love attention. You love attention. We just do. With spiritual things, if I can be made to appear more spiritual than you, then I may rationalize and justify my radical behavior as something Spirit-filled, when it is not. If we employ the same marketing strategies and sales techniques that the world does, it becomes very easy to work a crowd. It's even easier to work a Christian crowd because we, by design, are those who *want* to experience spiritual things. So, as a pastor, I have to be very careful about the line I walk. I don't want to find myself over in this camp, behaving in ways that aren't in the Word of God, but at the same time, I don't want to find myself in the camp that does not experience the fullness of God. If I look at the life of Christ and allow the Bible to be my guide, hopefully I will live my life as a Spirit-filled believer that will cause others to see what "Spirit-filled" looks like in a life and want the same for themselves. I want to be the kind of Christian that someone observes and says, "He's not like every other human being. He walks a slightly different path that I admire and respect. I wish I was in tune with the Spirit of God like he is." That's my prayer. That's also my prayer for the body of Christ. And I think this is the prayer you would also express. I think you would want to wake up in the morning and say, "God, make a difference with my life."

And you would want it to be the kind of difference that when the world watches you, although folks may not completely understand everything you do, certainly the fruit of what you do will bring praise and glory to God. This is what we all want. So why, then, is it something we don't all have? I am convinced it is because, in many cases, we truly don't understand this important doctrine on the Baptism of the Holy Spirit.

SMALL GROUP QUESTIONS

- What are some common misconceptions regarding the Baptism of the Holy Spirit?

- Where do these misconceptions come from?

- Why is it important to understand that Jesus was the most Spirit-filled man who ever lived?

- What are some extremes associated with the Baptism of the Holy Spirit, and why should we try to avoid them?

- How can we maintain the proper balance on this issue?

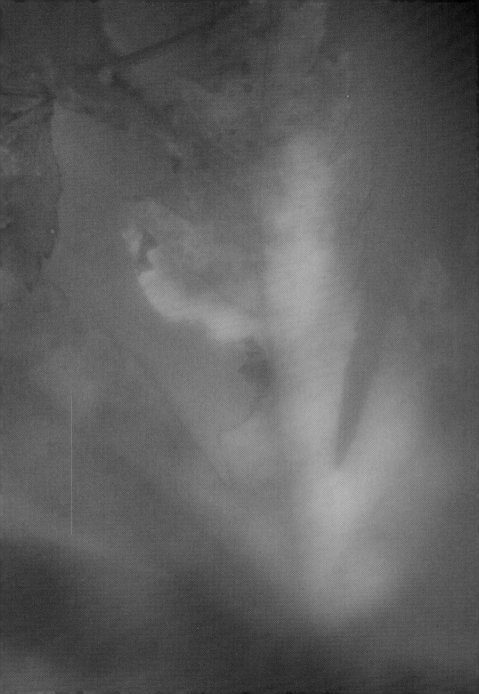

The Doctrine of the Holy Spirit

THE DOCTRINE OF THE HOLY SPIRIT

As a student of the Bible, when you sit down to study a doctrine, you need to locate the place in Scripture where the first mention of the doctrine appears and then follow its appearances throughout Scripture. As you follow it through, you will automatically develop your understanding of the doctrine. With this in mind, then, where in the Bible is the first mention of the Baptism of the Holy Spirit?

It's in the Gospel of John, in the first chapter, the 32nd verse:

(John 1:32-33 NKJV) And John bore witness, saying, "I saw the Spirit descending from heaven like a dove, and He remained upon Him. I did not know Him, but He who sent me to baptize with water said to me, 'Upon whom you see the Spirit descending, and remaining on Him, this is He who baptizes with the Holy Spirit.'"

John the Baptist was on a mission to find the Messiah. As

he started his search, the Spirit of God spoke to his heart and divinely debriefed him concerning this verse. God told John that he would know the Messiah because the Spirit, in the form of a dove, would light upon His body, and it is He who would baptize with the Spirit. Then John the Baptist experienced this just as the Word of God declares. He saw the dove descend upon Jesus, the Messiah.

Now, when it comes to this work of baptizing with the Spirit in verse 33, you may wonder where that occurs in Scripture. As we search the rest of Chapter 1 and Chapter 2, we come upon the first miracle, but no Baptism of the Holy Spirit. We read through Chapter 3 and meet Nicodemus, but still no mention of the Baptism of the Holy Spirit here; we move through Chapter 4 and encounter the woman at the well, but still nothing about Jesus baptizing in the Spirit; on to Chapter 5 – no, not there either; Chapter 6 – we are still looking for Jesus to baptize with the Holy Spirit, like God told John the Baptist He would – but it hasn't happened yet. So we search every word in Chapters 7 through 20, and nothing! We read John Chapter 21 through to verse 25. It ends, "Amen." All right. He didn't do it. I guess that ends this book. I mean, God told John that Jesus would baptize with the Holy Spirit, but John never saw it.

So, our next move is to find the subsequent place in Scripture where the phrase, "Baptism of the Holy Spirit,"

shows up again? Look with me now at Acts
1:4-5:

*(Acts 1:4-5 NKJV) And being assembled together with them,
He commanded them not to depart from Jerusalem, but to wait
for the Promise of the Father, "which," He said, "you have
heard from Me; for John truly baptized with water, but you
shall be baptized with the Holy Spirit not many days from
now."*

There it is. At this point, the disciples ask an earthly,
politically motivated question, which Jesus answers, and
then in verse eight, He declares:

*(Acts 1:8 NKJV) But you shall receive power when the Holy
Spirit has come upon you; and you shall be witnesses to Me in
Jerusalem, and in all Judea and Samaria, and to the end of the
earth."*

What is this? We now see that Jesus is prepared to
baptize with the Holy Spirit, but *when* does it happen? It
happens, in fact, after He has died and been glorified.
Why? Because this is when the Spirit comes "UPON" the
disciples to give them power to perform works of service.
This is not the Spirit coming "IN" the disciples to save
them. There is a distinct difference between the two.
Now, I know there are a lot of people who come from the
camp I referenced earlier who believe that when they got
saved they got as much of the Holy Spirit as they would

need for the rest of their life. Let me ask you this then. Why is it that the apostles, who also received the Holy Spirit "IN" them when they got saved were instructed by Jesus shortly thereafter to wait because they still needed to receive something additional - the Baptism of the Holy Spirit – before they could be witnesses for Jesus? Let's back up to the moment when the Twelve received the Spirit "IN" them. Go back just a page or two to John 20:19.

(John 20:19-22 NKJV) Then, the same day at evening, being the first day of the week, when the doors were shut where the disciples were assembled, for fear of the Jews, Jesus came and stood in the midst, and said to them, "Peace be with you." When He had said this, He showed them His hands and His side. Then the disciples were glad when they saw the Lord. So Jesus said to them again, "Peace to you! As the Father has sent Me, I also send you." And when He had said this, He breathed on them, and said to them, "Receive the Holy Spirit."

What did Jesus do? He breathed on them, and they all received the Spirit. I need to point out the obvious – it is Jesus giving the Spirit. If anyone else was giving the Spirit, I would wonder, "Maybe they didn't get the Spirit and that's why they still needed it in Acts 1:8, because if it was someone else breathing on them, you don't know if they would really get the Spirit because who has the Spirit to give?" It's Jesus who has the Spirit to give, so when He says, "Receive the Holy Spirit," you have to

know they got it! But what exactly did they get here in
John 20:22? They got the indwelling Spirit for salvation.
This is that moment when the disciples are saved.

You may be thinking, wait a second. Didn't the disciples
get saved when they first started following the Lord?
They couldn't have, at least not in the New Testament
sense. In the Old Testament sense, certainly they were
following Christ the way Abraham followed Christ, the
same way Noah followed Christ. But they couldn't have
followed Christ in the New Testament sense, not yet,
because Christ had not yet died and been glorified. Let
me explain it from the Scriptures. Go to John 7:37-39.

*(John 7:37-39 NKJV) On the last day, that great day of the
feast, Jesus stood and cried out, saying, "If anyone thirsts, let
him come to Me and drink. He who believes in Me, as the
Scripture has said, out of his heart will flow rivers of living
water." But this He spoke concerning the Spirit, whom those
believing in Him would receive; for the Holy Spirit was not yet
given, because Jesus was not yet glorified.*

What is the problem here? The problem is that Jesus
could not offer salvation in the New Testament sense
until He had conquered hell and death. After He had
conquered hell and death, the first order of business for
Him was to get together with His disciples and impart the
Holy Spirit for salvation through indwelling. But then He
said to them shortly thereafter, if I may paraphrase for

"But you shall receive power
when the Holy Spirit has
come upon you; and
you shall be witnesses
to Me in Jerusalem,
and in all Judea and Samaria,
and to the end of the earth."

ACTS 1:8 NKJV

you: "I don't want you to take one step out of Jerusalem until you are endued from on high. You need some additional spiritual power to come "UPON" you. This is not the Spirit coming "IN" you; this is the Spirit coming "UPON" you. I don't want you to do anything until you have the Spirit coming "UPON" you. Do you understand?"

The disciples got it because they waited, and they waited, and they tarried, and they prayed. In the book of Acts in the second chapter, the Spirit came upon them, and immediately a transformation, a complete change, took place in their lives and in their ministries. It is so glorious that Peter, who at one time was vehemently and fearfully denying Christ, now - with the Spirit's power upon him - is dynamically and fearlessly preaching Christ. And it is not the indwelling Spirit that made the difference, because even after receiving the Holy Spirit for indwelling salvation in John 20:22, Peter still remained trembling in the upper room, afraid of being taken by the soldiers. Here, in Acts 2, with the Spirit's power upon him, he is boldly and unashamedly preaching Christ, and 3,000 people got saved in that one Bible study! Something definitely happened to Peter.

Let's find out what happened not only to Peter, but what can happen to us. Look at John 14:17.

(John 14:17 NKJV) *"..the Spirit of truth, whom the world*

cannot receive, because it neither sees Him nor knows Him; but you know Him, for He dwells with you and will be in you."

The word for "with" in the original language is the Greek word, *para*. It means "alongside." It describes the way the Spirit works in your life before you come to Christ. Do you remember that before you actually asked Jesus into your life the Spirit was knocking? For some of you, the Spirit was banging. You could not deny the fact that you were hearing God speak to your heart. When and how did it happen? Perhaps, it happened at the birth of your first child. You really didn't acknowledge God as God, but something occurred when your baby came out of the womb and the nurse placed that tiny life in your arms for the very first time, and you thought, "You know what? This is a miracle!" And with tears flowing down your face, you cried, "There must be a God because right now I feel His presence." It happened for me at the birth of both my kids. The minute they came out of the womb and I held them in my arms, I sensed the presence of God in a magnificent and glorious way that I had not felt in all my Christian experience up to that point.

Maybe, instead, it happened for you at the death of a friend. You went to the funeral, and the pastor was teaching from the Bible on eternal life. As he began to talk about the future and the Kingdom of God where there will be no more weeping, no more pain, and no more sorrow, you thought, "That sounds like a great place to spend my eternity."

Both these experiences are examples of moments when the Spirit was coming alongside you and saying, "Come here. Come on." Each time there was a knock – I had a baby, it made me think about God. Knock knock. My friend died, it made me think a little bit more about God. Knock knock. There was this guy who handed me this little book on the Baptism of the Holy Spirit. Knock knock.

You are reading this book for a reason. Something has been happening in your life over the last couple of months, maybe over the last couple of weeks, that is drawing you closer and closer to God. That is the *para* work of the Spirit.

The next step, in the words of Jesus, is "You know Him, and He dwells with you (*para*), now He will be *in* you." In the Greek, the word for "in" is *en*. What Jesus was saying is that the Holy Spirit right then was alongside the disciples, but pretty soon He would actually come in them. That is what happened in John 20:22 when Jesus declared, "Receive the Holy Spirit." In that moment, the Holy Spirit came into the disciples, and they received the indwelling Holy Spirit. But then Jesus told them not to take even one step in ministry responsibility until the Holy Spirit had come upon them. Look again at Acts 1:8.

(Acts 1:8 NKJV) "But you shall receive power when the Holy Spirit has come upon you; and you shall be witnesses to Me in Jerusalem, and in all Judea and Samaria, and to the end of the earth."

That word for "upon" - it is *epi* in the Greek. What happens in your life when the Spirit comes upon you? This verse says you will receive power and you will become witnesses. The word for power in the Greek is *dunamis,* and it is where we get our English word "dynamite." This is explosive power. When the Holy Spirit comes upon you, it is explosive. It is so powerful that you are willing to be a witness. A witness? Yes. This word in the Greek is *martus,* or "martyr" in English. When the Holy Spirit comes upon you, you are so filled with the Spirit that you are willing to die for the faith. That's what happened to Cassie Bernell at the 1999 Columbine High School massacre in Colorado. Some of us wondered if we had been in her shoes and someone pointed a gun at our head, asking, "Do you believe in God?" if we would have demonstrated this girl's courage and faith. There are many of us that would have just stayed silent. In fact, there was another girl, crawling on the floor, who was asked that same question, and she said that because her mind was so shattered in fear, she didn't know how to respond. She stayed hidden under a table in the same library. She couldn't answer. Cassie, on the other hand, was able to proclaim her faith in Christ and be martyred for it.

Would I be bold enough to stand up for my faith as Cassie did? Am I so unashamed of the gospel that when someone points a gun in my face and screams, "Do you believe in Jesus?" I could answer, "Yes, I believe in Jesus!" What a profound, truth-revealing second set apart in eternity!

Is the key issue here whether we have the power to die for Jesus and testify of His greatness in the face of death? No, I think the more important question for us is, "Do we have the power to live for Him and testify of His greatness in the face of ridicule and scorn?"

Tomorrow, can you actually go to your workplace, set your Bible down, open it up, and walk away, and if someone comes by and says, "Hey, what's that? You got a Bible on your desk?" can you turn around and say, "Yeah. Do you have any questions about Christianity? I have some answers"? Does that thought freak you out? So many of us, when it comes to our Christian faith in the workplace, think we can be secret agents for God. Oh, we have a Bible; it's one of those pocket-sized ones that fits neatly in our drawer. We wait until our lunch break, take the key, and unlock it, clandestinely sneaking peeks in between watching to make sure no one sees us. Then we pathetically say, "Thank You, Lord, for my verse of the day." Or, we are at the water cooler and our coworkers are talking about their weekend. They turn to us and say, "Hey, what did you do?" "Well, I uh . . . went to . . uh . .

church......," we mumble. "You went where?" "Church." "I didn't hear you, get your fingers out of your mouth. Where did you go, what did you do with the weekend?" We are ashamed to even say we went to church, let alone tell anyone the Good News about Jesus.

What's the problem? No power! But when the Spirit comes upon you, you get dynamite power. You are willing to be a witness and die for the Lord, if need be, and you're equally willing to live your life for the Lord. When someone asks you about Christianity, you'll step right up to the plate and talk about it.

If you don't have that Holy Spirit power, you might say, "Well, yes, I went to church. I think the church is a nice organization, and I went this weekend and. . . I kind of . . . well . . . liked it." Then you quickly change the subject, "Did you see any good movies this weekend? Did you see that movie, "The Dark Knight"? Let me just say - that kind of Christianity won't attract or change anybody. As a human, I am not interested. I respect and admire people who do things full-volume. I think that's why we watch marathon runners. We look at them and say, "Those guys are going to run how many miles?" We admire them because we know they are totally sold out. We respect them because they are willing to give their all to whatever they take on. If a man is so shy concerning what he believes that he is not even willing to display his faith or testify about it, our reaction is typically, "No thanks. I don't want to be like you. Sounds to me like you have a hard time with Christianity yourself. Don't you? Don't you?! And you want me to buy it? I don't think so. I don't need another thing in my life that doesn't work or won't make a difference."

SMALL GROUP QUESTIONS

- Where is the Baptism of the Holy Spirit first mentioned in Scripture?

- What is the difference between the Spirit coming "in" and coming "upon" a person?

- How was this difference demonstrated in the disciples' lives?

- Are there evidences of the Spirit's baptism in your life? If so, what are they?

- What are some negative consequences of not experiencing the Baptism of the Holy Spirit?

SET APART FOR SERVICE

How can we be different? We can be different through this very doctrine that we have been talking about. We can get the Spirit of God to come "IN" us through salvation and then pray and ask for the Spirit of God to come "UPON" us for works of service. That means that the Spirit of God for service is a different dynamic operating in a different dimension. With God's Spirit for service, we will see a depth, a witness, and a power in our life. Not until we have been baptized with God's Spirit in this *"epi"* experience will we know the dynamite power of God's Spirit that enables us to become witnesses who are willing to die, if need be, for the faith.

This transformation is best displayed in Peter's life. We touched on it earlier, but go back again to John 20. You cannot help but see this. What is the first act the disciples perform as Christians after receive the indwelling Holy Spirit for salvation in John 20? The answer is here in John 21:3. Now that they have the Holy Spirit, the first thing they do is…ready for this?

(John 21:3 NKJV) Simon Peter said to them, "I am going fishing."

WHAT??? Yeah, he's going fishing! "Hey, guys, anyone want to go fishing?" Now, why is that so comical? It's comical because this is the very thing that comes naturally to Peter. He is a fisherman. For him to say right now that he wants to go fishing means that even though he has received the Holy Spirit for salvation, he is still inclined to go on doing what is natural for him to do. Nothing has really changed in Peter's life, even with the indwelling Spirit for salvation. The disciples join Peter, and they, too, do what comes naturally, i.e. go fishing. But they fish all night and catch nothing. Look at the second half of verse 3:

(John 21:3b NKJV) They went out and immediately got into the boat, and that night they caught nothing.

So, not only is Peter back to doing what is natural for him, he is not even successful at it until Jesus shows up on the scene. When Jesus shows up, in verse 5, He says, if I might paraphrase, "Hey, kids, got any food?" "No, we don't," they reply. "Well," continues Jesus, "why don't you cast your net on the other side of the boat?"

Now, I don't know if you can catch how tongue-in-cheek Jesus is being in this statement. Here He is, standing on the shore, and there's Peter in the boat with the disciples. If you are a fisherman, you look at someone on shore as a "landlubber." So here is a "landlubber" telling them how to fish. Jesus' fishing advice is even more humorous. He tells them to put their net on the other side of the boat, as if on one side of the boat there are no fish, but on the other side of the boat there is plenty of fish. How big would this boat have to be to make that kind of difference? I mean…really! You can imagine at this point that Peter wants to shout, "Hey, buddy, leave me alone. All right?" Do you understand how comical this is? This is something you might do to play a trick on someone you are taking out fishing for the very first time. While the guy has his pole on one side of the boat and catching nothing, you say, "Hey, put your pole on the other side, that's where all the fish are." Quite naively he says, "Oh. Reeeaally? Oh, O.K." A true fisherman would find the absurdity of this hilarious. He would be rolling with sarcastic hysteria. "Yeah, right. The fish are on the other side of the boat." Can you imagine? I mean, come on, the distance beneath the boat is about two feet. If they are not on one side, they are certainly not on the other side. Give me a break.

Perhaps, Peter remembered an earlier time when he was casting his net for fish and Jesus called out to him, "Follow Me, and I will make you become fishers of men" (Mark 1:17) and, now in a strange *déjà vu* moment, he looked over at the Man on the shore, not recognizing Him, but surrendering nonetheless: "Who is that? Hey, guys, let's throw the net on the other side and see what happens. Yeah, on the other side. Just do it, all right?" As they try and draw up the net, they have a difficult

"Follow Me,
and I will make
you become
fishers of men"

MARK 1:17 NKJV

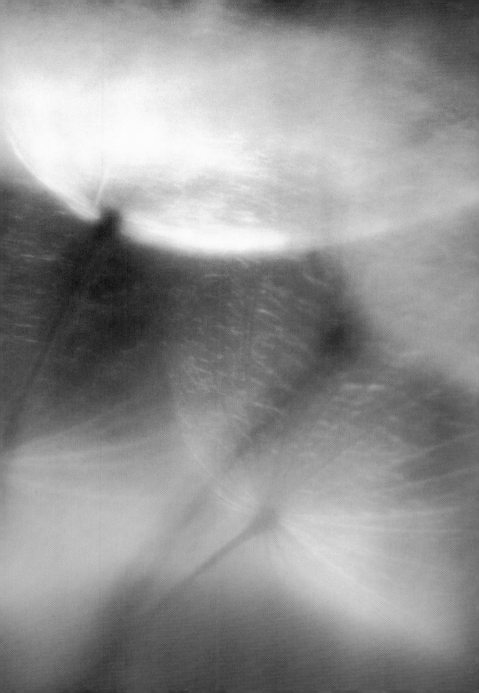

time getting it into the boat because of the abundant
bounty of fish. I am sure at this point that it is Jesus who
is rolling with hysteria on the seashore.

This was a test for the disciples. Jesus wanted to find out
how obedient they were going to be. He knows that they
have the indwelling Spirit for salvation, but when it
comes to works of service, He will tell them to tarry and
wait, and when the Spirit comes upon them, they will
find themselves exploding with power to serve in a
capacity that will break the nets of their wildest
imagination.

Think about it. Peter is a Christian, saved, and indwelt by
the Holy Spirit. He goes out fishing and catches nothing.
Yet once Peter is filled with the Spirit in Acts 2, he goes
out fishing for men, and in his first sermon he preaches a
message so powerful that 3,000 people get saved in one
day. Please don't think that there is no difference in
Peter's life. Of course there is.

God is painting a picture for us of the power that
transforms the life of the believer for works of service
through the Baptism of the Holy Spirit. We see it
theoretically here, and we also see it theologically.
Take a theological look with me for a moment at the
churches in the United States of America today. Notice
the ones that embrace the doctrine of the Baptism of the
Holy Spirit and look at the work they are doing - who is
getting saved, how are they getting saved, and how are
their lives being changed?

SMALL GROUP QUESTIONS

- What was the significance of Peter's decision to go fishing?

- How did Jesus test the disciples by telling them to throw their nets over the other side of the boat? Why did He do it?

- What lesson can be learned by comparing Peter's inability to catch any fish with what he does in Acts Chapter 2?

- What trend typically materializes in churches that embrace the Spirit's baptism?

- What happens in churches that don't?

Now, look at the churches that do not embrace this
doctrine of the Baptism of the Holy Spirit, and you will
notice that many are closing their doors, selling their
buildings, and shutting down their ministry. There is not
that Spirit of power. Do you understand why?

If I get up tomorrow morning and say, "God, baptize me
afresh today with Your Spirit; I want to be led by You; I
want to be guided by You," I will find myself going into
an adventure mode. It is in that adventure mode that my
Christianity becomes exciting and electric. It becomes
relevant to where and how I live that day of my life. It
gives me the boldness to say, "I am going to do
something a little bit different today. I won't even take
the same route to work because I sense God's Spirit
leading me a different way." Then, on that different
route, I find a lost soul needing ministry. I have been
filled with God's Spirit for ministry and connected by
God's sovereign hand to fulfill the need in another's life.
There is no comparison to the joy this brings in the heart
of a believer.

On the other hand, if I am conservative when it comes to
spiritual things and somewhat hesitant to let anything
disrupt my day, I will follow a planned program for my
life - the same way I follow a program at church. Every
day and every thing are always the same. Life is routine,
rote, and religious. I know what I am going to eat for
dinner on Tuesday night. I know what we are going to
watch on television on Thursday night. I'm talking about
Christians here. There is no dynamic of anything
spiritual, anything miraculous, or anything out of the
ordinary happening in their lives for the simple reason
that they have programmed their path to be predictable.
They couldn't conceive of taking anything but the same
route to work. To follow the road less taken would be
living on the cutting edge for them. Come on! Please. If
you do take the same route to work everyday – spice it
up!! Do something a little bold! Live on the wild side
tomorrow and take a new road! Then, on your way to
work, you just might notice a car broken down. In it is a
precious, elderly woman, with her head up against the
steering wheel in desperation praying, "God, I am scared
to death. I cannot believe I got a flat tire. Please send me
an angel, Lord. Please send someone to change my tire. I
don't know how to do it. I don't even know where the
jack is. I can't get the tire off. God, I am afraid. I am in a
city I don't know and don't want to be in. Please, God."

Suddenly there is a tap on her window. It's you. You are
her angel. How did that happen? You simply woke up

in the morning and said, "God, fill me with Your Spirit. Lead me and guide me. I don't want it to be same-old, same-old. I want to be in touch with You, Lord." So God changes your route, and you run into this ministry waiting to happen. You know this is your divine appointment. "Excuse me," you say. She looks up and is startled. "Hello, can I help you out?" She says, "Well, I'm a . . ." And then you say this, "I prayed this morning, and I believe God led me here to help you out." She begins to shake and says, "You are my answer to prayer. Praise the Lord!" WOW! Now the Spirit connects and you grab that jack and start to serve with an enthusiasm and strength that is borne of those divine times when heaven touches earth, and you are the ground wire! It is electrifying.

This is Christianity. This is what is supposed to be happening in our lives every single day. What happens too often, though, is that we wake up in the morning and it *is* the same-old, same-old. The Spirit knocks, and we shrug Him off. "Not right now. I am listening to the radio, and I like this person who's talking." He knocks a little harder on your heart and says, "Well, I don't care for crass radio personality, why don't you shut it off?" You see, we can do the same thing that the world does. We can drive to church and be bored, bothered, and bugged by everything that happens. Or we can open our hearts to the Spirit and pray. We can communicate with the Lord and find out who the people are that He wants us to

"Now when the apostles
who were at Jerusalem heard that
Samaria had received the word of God,
they sent Peter and John to them,
who, when they had come down,
prayed for them that they might
receive the Holy Spirit.
For as yet He had fallen
upon none of them.
They had only been baptized
in the name of the Lord Jesus.
Then they laid hands on them,
and they received the Holy Spirit."

ACTS 8:14-17 NKJV

pray for. The next time you are in a traffic jam, don't get mad. Be glad that God might give you an opportunity to pray for the person in the car next to you. You don't know!!! But you will never know unless you open your heart to God's Spirit. He wants to do these kinds of things in your daily life.

We do a disservice to the Christian faith when we live in a world we know nothing about. In your hometown, chances are there is a New Age bookstore. You can walk into that bookstore, and you can find out how to leave your body by astral projecting your brain and spirit somewhere else, how to travel around in demon circles, and how to come back again. Yet, we, who have the real Spirit, who have the living God Himself to lead and guide us – when He knocks on our heart and says, "Hey, a little something different today?" - we have the audacity to say, "No, no, no. It's got to be the same." I am sure His heart breaks at our answer. He sees people in occult circles adventurous, traveling, in seances, trying to raise the dead, and we are so stuck in our conservative, comfortable, predictable mindsets that we find the very topic of the Baptism of the Holy Spirit way beyond our comfort zone.

As you read about the apostle Peter's transformation as a result of the Baptism of the Holy Spirit upon his life, you might find yourself questioning this extraordinary event. But what if it happens again and again in Scripture?

What if, over and over again, you read about people who are saved, getting prayed for, and then receive the Holy Spirit coming upon them? It's right there in Acts Chapter 8.

(Acts 8:14-17 NKJV) Now when the apostles who were at Jerusalem heard that Samaria had received the word of God, they sent Peter and John to them, who, when they had come down, prayed for them that they might receive the Holy Spirit. For as yet He had fallen upon none of them. They had only been baptized in the name of the Lord Jesus. Then they laid hands on them, and they received the Holy Spirit.

What exactly is happening here? The apostles had come upon some people in Samaria who had received the Word of God and had been baptized in the name of Jesus, but the Spirit had not yet come upon *(epi)* them. They were baptized into Jesus, which is being baptized into the faith, through salvation. Now they are being prayed for to receive the Holy Spirit for works of service.

In this passage of Scripture there is a difference between the two baptisms. That difference becomes clear when we understand the meaning of the word "baptism." We actually find several baptisms being taught in Scripture. There is a *Baptism* into Moses, a *Baptism* with fire, a *Baptism* by water, a *Baptism* into the faith. These all employ the same word because there is only one word in the Greek for baptism. It means to submerge or immerse for religious purposes. Calvary Chapel embraces the practice of dunking rather than sprinkling for this reason. When we dunk those being baptized under the water, we can achieve the fullest extent of the meaning of baptism. They are being immersed, submerged, drenched, saturated.

When we apply this same definition to the events in Acts 8, we find a group of believers that are drenched and immersed into the doctrine of Jesus Christ but that have not yet been drenched and immersed into the doctrine of the Holy Spirit. How did they achieve this? It came about when the apostles laid hands on them and prayed for their Baptism by the Holy Spirit; then suddenly the Holy Spirit came upon them. We also find this happening in Acts 19.

(Acts 19:1-6 NKJV) And it happened, while Apollos was at Corinth, that Paul, having passed through the upper regions, came to Ephesus. And finding some disciples (believers in Jesus Christ) *he said to them, "Did you receive the Holy Spirit when you believed?" So they said to him, "We have not so much as heard whether there is a Holy Spirit." And he said to them, "Into what then were you baptized?" So they said, "Into John's baptism." Then Paul said, "John indeed baptized with a baptism of repentance, saying to the people that they should believe on Him who would come after him, that is, on Christ Jesus." When they heard this, they were baptized in the name of the Lord Jesus. And when Paul had laid hands on them, the Holy Spirit came upon them, and they spoke with tongues and prophesied.*

Not that you need any more clarification, but we find yet another example of the Baptism of the Holy Spirit in the conversion of Saul, after he becomes Paul, in Acts 9:10-18. Keep in mind that Paul is already a believer, but it is not until he comes to the house of Ananias, and Ananias lays his hands on "brother" Saul and the Holy Spirit comes upon him that he becomes the apostle Paul.

SMALL GROUP QUESTIONS

- How can a Spirit-filled perspective impact one's daily routine?

- What bearing does the Spirit's baptism have on the way we interact with our world?

- What does the word "baptism" actually mean?

- When was the last time the Holy Spirit led you to do something spontaneous and exciting?

- What were the long-term results of following the Spirit's lead?

THE ISSUE OF TONGUES

Now, if you can see this doctrine clearly displayed in Acts 9, in Acts 8, and in Acts 19, at some point you have to sense the scales tipping away from your predisposed prejudice in favor of an acceptance of the truth of God's Word. Even with all this evidence, however, there are times when we still don't want to embrace the doctrine of the Baptism of the Holy Spirit. Why not? Sadly enough, it is because of what happened in the last half of Acts 19:6:

*(Acts 19:6 NKJV) And when Paul had laid hands on them, the Holy Spirit came upon them, **and they spoke with tongues and prophesied.***

Oh boy. This is the thing that has the church of Jesus Christ undone! This is the bath water, in which the baby sits, that you want to throw out. You are sure that if you were to open your heart to this doctrine you would become one of those wacky "tongue talkers." You are simply not ready for that. Up to this point, perhaps you were starting to consider the possibility of empowerment from God's Spirit, but not at the expense of looking like an idiot.

What are you really afraid of? You may say, "Well, the whole idea of speaking in tongues – I have heard about that stuff; I have even heard that they were doing it at that same church where my friend's relative went. They actually tried to teach him to talk in tongues. They grabbed hold of his tongue and wiggled it back and forth. They gave him sentences to repeat, trying to get him "jump started." They said, "Say this after me – 'my,'" and he said, "my." "Mamma," "mamma," "gotta," "gotta," "new," "new," "honda," "honda." Then they said, "Now say it really fast – "My momma gotta new Honda." "Mymommagottanewhonda. Mymommagottanewhonda." "That's it! You got it." "Mama la onda, shondalaa oohla." Yeah, right. Talk about a real work of the flesh. Stop it!

On the other hand, if speaking in tongues is what the Bible says it is, then it is supernatural; it is spiritual; and, even more so, it is scriptural. Please keep in mind that the true evidence of being baptized in the Holy Spirit is not tongues but power. That's right, power. That is the first evidence. It is so important to stress this point because the one thing the church of today seems to be missing is that *dunamis* power that turned the world of the first century church upside down, not talking in tongues. I realize that the apostle Paul wanted everyone to talk in tongues, but not at the expense of the division that today has taken its toll in loss of power.

When I was a new believer, just a few weeks old in the Lord, I did not understand this doctrine. For that reason,

I, even as an extrovert, was a bit timid, specifically on spiritual things. So, in the first few weeks after I was saved, when someone would ask me about Jesus, I became extremely uncomfortable. I felt shame because of how serious a sinner I had been. I did not even feel comfortable sitting in church, let alone telling anyone about Jesus. I felt so unholy and was convinced that I was not worthy to even mention Jesus, so for me to talk to anyone about Him was just not going to happen. My brother picked up on this, and a few weeks after my salvation experience, he sat me down and said, "Bob, you know what you need? You need the Baptism of the Holy Spirit." At that point in time, being so new in the faith, I didn't have a chance to have my mind tainted by somebody telling me that there was no such thing, so I said, "Well, what is it?" He answered, "Let me show you." Then he basically took me through this same doctrine that I am teaching you today. Afterward, he asked me, "Do you want to receive the Baptism of the Holy Spirit?" And I said, "Well, it seems pretty clear here, so, yeah, of course I do." So he, his wife, and I started praying right there on his living room floor. I still remember my brother's prayer. "Lord, I believe You have a special gift for Bob today, the Baptism of your Holy Spirit. . ." Then he started to kind of shake a little bit, and his wife started to wiggle a little. I kind of looked on and noticed that I was not wiggling at all. I thought to myself, "Is there an earthquake in Nevada I don't know about? Is something going on here?" Then he said to me, "Now you pray." So I prayed, "Lord, baptize me with Your Spirit. I want to be filled with Your Holy Spirit. I want to be empowered by You." When we finished praying, I said, "Hey, I noticed you and Theresa shook a little bit. Everything all right?" He said, "Oh, yeah, I just kind of felt something." I said, "Why didn't I feel anything?" He said, "Bob, God treats every one of us unique to our own personality. Some people will feel like this warm syrup on their heads; other people don't feel a thing, but it is by faith, not feeling, that we walk in our Christian experience." I said, "Oh, O.K." Then he said, "But now watch what happens in your life." Sure enough, it happened. About two days later, I was in a grocery store line, and there was a woman in front of me. She was one of those people you spot from time to time in life that just look like they are carrying a burden. I was right there behind her, and I had my cart, and I was looking at her. Now, remember, at this point in time I was still seriously shy about spiritual things, and I was in no way planning on saying anything to her about the Lord. All of a sudden, however, after praying this prayer at my brother's house two days earlier, there were words moving around in my mouth. No – it was not tongues – it was English. O.K.? English! I didn't blast her with Mymammagottanewhonda! No, no, no. It wasn't like that at all.

In Galatians 5:22 and 23, Paul tells us that the fruit of the Spirit is love, joy, peace, patience, kindness, goodness, faithfulness, gentleness, and self-control. Let me underscore the "self-control" part of this biblical truth for the sake of this lesson. Those who are baptized in God's Spirit do not have to fear being in a bank line somewhere and suddenly having to plead with God, "Oh, no, Lord, not here, not now!" as they are being overtaken by some wild spirit that is about to compel them to fall on the floor, writhing and screaming out non-intelligible words. This does not happen in a believer's life that is filled with God's Spirit because one fruit of that same Spirit is self-control. That's why the Bible states:

(1 Corinthians 14:32 NLT) Remember that people who prophesy are in control of their spirit and can wait their turn.

In other words, we don't lose control of our actions once we are baptized in the Holy Spirit.

Here's the first way that the Baptism of the Holy Spirit displayed itself in my case. When that sad-looking lady in the grocery line in front of me left the store, I followed after her. I didn't have that many groceries. I was single at the time, and all I had was ketchup. (That's all you need as a single person – you open up the fridge, and as long as you have ketchup and mustard, you're fine.) I went up to her, and I said, "Excuse me. You are really troubled with something right now and could use some prayer, right?" She looked at me and began to cry and spill her guts to me. I realized that this was a serious need so I took time to pray with her.

What happened next still blows my mind. I started getting Bible verses in the back of my brain that at one time I had read but I had no idea that I knew. God's Spirit began feeding me the information on the spot,

"And when Paul
had laid hands on them, the
Holy Spirit came upon them,
and they spoke with
tongues and prophesied."

ACTS 19:6 NKJV

giving me revelation so I had something to say to this woman who was hurting. She told me that I was saying to her the very thing she needed to hear. I walked away from her, thinking, "Wow. That was very cool, very cool – Baptism of the Spirit. Yeah, now I get it."

Next thing you know, I was at the drive-thru at McDonalds. The guy says, "What do you want?" I said, "I want everyone in McDonalds to get saved, that's what I want." No, I didn't really. But what I did do was start carrying Bible tracts with me and at every drive-thru I went to, I exchanged the food for a little tract and would say something like, "Hey, I just want to tell you something. If you read this or not, it is not as important as you just being reminded today that God loves you very, very much and has a plan for your life." Nothing profound, just something friendly, something kind. I noticed that it wasn't any time at all before the cashiers started looking forward to my visits. I progressed right into asking them if I could pray with them. Suddenly, I was operating in a realm of spirituality that I had not been in before. This is what God wants us all to have because this is our Christian witness in the real world. This spiritual power to be witnesses is what makes us different.

Allow me to prove my point. Look at Ephesians 5, wherein the apostle Paul gives us an exhortation. Keep in mind this is being written to the church in Ephesus. This is a church. These are Christians.

(Ephesians 5:18-25 NKJV) And do not be drunk with wine, in which is dissipation; but be filled with the Spirit, speaking to one another in psalms and hymns and spiritual songs, singing and making melody in your heart to the Lord, giving thanks always for all things to God the Father in the name of our Lord Jesus Christ, submitting to one another in the fear of God. Wives, submit to your own husbands, as to the Lord. For the husband is head of the wife, as also Christ is head of the church; and He is the Savior of the body. Therefore, just as the church is subject to Christ, so let the wives be to their own husbands in everything. Husbands, love your wives, just as Christ also loved the church and gave Himself for her...

I must admit that, as a believer, I have often mistakenly presented the guidelines and ground rules for marriage without the prerequisite for accomplishing them. If I say to every wife in this room, "Now, women, you know how you should behave. You have to be submissive to your husbands," I am going to automatically meet with resistance, defiance, and rebellion unless the woman is Spirit-filled. But, if a woman is Spirit-filled, she has the kind of power to be a witness – a martyr – to live out what's right; she has power to submit. But without the Holy Spirit, I don't think a woman can submit in her own flesh. In the same way, I can say to guys, "Hey, guys, love your wives as Christ loved the church and gave Himself up for her. It is time to live sacrificially for the sake of someone else." Let me tell you something, there is not a man on this earth that wants to do that unless he has the power of the Holy Spirit. But, if he does have the

power of the Holy Spirit in his life, then he says, "O.K. I
want to do what God tells me to do."

SMALL GROUP QUESTIONS

* Why do tongues tend to be such an intimidating topic?

* What is the true evidence of the Spirit's baptism in a
  person's life?

* How would you explain the relationship between the
  fruit of the Spirit in Galatians 5:22-23 and the gift of
  tongues?

* Why is the misuse of this gift so potentially dangerous?

* What is your own attitude toward tongues, and does it
  align with Scripture

What do Paul's words in Ephesians 5:18, "be filled with the Spirit," mean? In every language on earth, there are verbs, or action words. Verbs have tenses and moods. When we understand the tense or mood of a verb in a particular phrase or passage, it speaks all the more to the meaning of the communication. Let's look at the phrase from Ephesians in the above verse and make a few interesting observations.

1. The verb "be" in Paul's phrase, "be filled," is in the present tense. This is noteworthy because some people believe that the operation of spiritual gifts ended with the conclusion of the apostolic age. They will explain that the apostles needed the power of the gifts, but once we received the Word of God, we did not need the power of the gifts anymore. Are they serious? Can you honestly say that the church does not need power today? Where did they get this?

    Well, doesn't the Bible say that tongues will cease,

prophecy will cease, that all these things will cease?
Yes, it does, but when? When "perfect" has come, the
Bible says. Now those in the camp that say the
spiritual gifts are not for today believe that "perfect"
is the Word of God. I take issue with that. I believe
that the "perfect" referred to here is none other than
Jesus Christ. I think that when Jesus Christ comes
back again, you're right, there will be no more need
for tongues, prophecy, or any of the other spiritual
gifts. Right now, however, the church needs all the
power it can get, and the Bible bears this out because
the verb is in the present tense. Another reason I can
say this so confidently is because when all the
townspeople were baptized with the Holy Spirit that
very first time, and they wondered, "What is this?"
the apostle Peter stood up boldly and answered, "This
is what was spoken of by the prophet Joel who said:
'And it shall come to pass afterward That I will pour
out My Spirit on all flesh; Your sons and daughters
shall prophesy, Your old men shall dream dreams,
Your young men shall see visions'" (Joel 2:28). As
Peter tells them this, he takes them from the beginning
of the end to the very, very end of the end when the
moon and sun are changed to darkness and blood.
He didn't say, "This pouring out of the Spirit is for
right now, then it will stop, and then it will be the
end." No, instead, he told them that the pouring out
of the Spirit was for then and that it would continue
until the very end of the age. That is the meaning of
the present tense.

2. The phrase "be filled" can also be understood in a continuous present connotation. The meaning now is that we are not filled just once, but rather that we are always being filled. In other words, "be filled" also carries the meaning, "keep on being filled with the Holy Spirit."

   Why do we sincerely need to grasp the meaning of the phrase in this context? Because Christians, wherever they live, wherever they walk, they all leak. Did you know that? I can get filled with the Holy Spirit at a Tuesday evening Bible study, but come Wednesday morning, I am drained, barely alive spiritually. We need to be filled each and every morning with God's Spirit. When we wake up and are empty, we need to go to God for a fresh filling of His Spirit.

3. The phrase "be filled" is also in the imperative mood, directed to a plural subject. It is not like the apostle Paul is saying, "Hey, you know what? I think it would be a really good idea if you guys were Spirit-filled." That's not what he is saying at all. He is saying, "Be filled! You must be filled!" He is issuing a command, and because his command is in the plural in the original language, it means that it applies to every Christian.

4. The phrase "be filled" is also in the passive voice. In passive voice constructions, the subject is a recipient.

"be filled with the Spirit"

EPHESIANS 5:18 NKJV

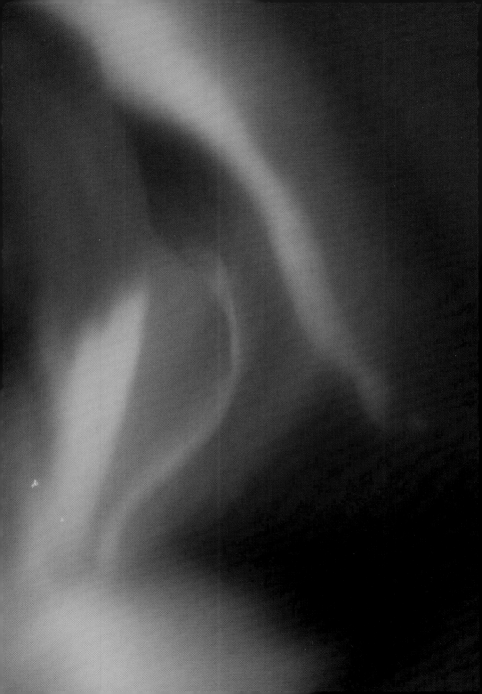

It is acted upon. It does not perform the action; it is the destination of the action. Not all verbs can be put into the passive voice. Take the verb "run," for example. You cannot use "run" in the passive voice because it is only an active verb; the subject of the sentence is the only one doing the running; the subject cannot be the receiver of the action of running – it doesn't make any sense. But this verb phrase, "be filled," in Ephesians 5:18, understood in its passive voice connotation, means that it is not something I do or have to work up. I can't fill myself. On the contrary, I need to allow the Spirit to fill me. When Paul tells us to be filled with the Spirit, he is not telling us to go out and fill ourselves; he is telling us to allow this work of the Spirit to take hold in us. In other words, at the end of one of my teachings, I can't start hollering, "And howwww about YOUUUUU! DO YOUUUU WANT TO GET BAPTIZED IN THE HOLY SPIRIT? NOW TODAY!" I could really work it up and get you all worked up, too, but I would be phony, I'd be fake, I'd be pretending. I believe that those of you who are wise would know it. You would sit here for a few minutes, watch the shenanigans, the sensationalism, watch me on the stage, and then say, "You know what? Bob's changed. He's not real anymore. He's bought into some weird doctrine, and I don't like it." You get the idea.

SMALL GROUP QUESTIONS

- Is the Spirit's filling as necessary today as it was in New Testament times?

- When will spiritual gifts no longer be necessary? Why?

- Why is it so important to be filled with the Holy Spirit on a continual basis?

- Who does the command, "Be filled with the Spirit" apply to?

- What is the significance of this command being in the passive voice?

CONSIDER THE CLAIMS

Here is what I am going to do. I gave you the doctrine.
Now you go home, kneel down next to your bed, and
pray that God would baptize you with His Spirit so that
you can live in a different dynamic, filled with spiritual
power. You do that all on your own - you don't need me
involved. God will answer your prayer because He is
faithful to His Word.

Now, if any one of you reading this is concerned that you
might be opening up yourself to some foreign, wild,
demonic spirit if you look up to heaven and pray, "Lord,
may Your Spirit come upon me," turn to Luke 11.

*(Luke 11:11-13 NKJV) "If a son asks for bread from any father
among you, will he give him a stone? Or if he asks for a fish,
will he give him a serpent instead of a fish? Or if he asks for an
egg, will he offer him a scorpion? If you then, being evil, know
how to give good gifts to your children, how much more will
your heavenly Father give the Holy Spirit to those who ask
Him!"*

Do you understand the mindset Jesus Christ is presenting to us? He is saying, in essence, "How dare you for a moment think that if you are humble of heart, with an open spirit, and you cry out to God, 'Lord, I want a fresh filling of Your Holy Spirit,' that He is going to be up there in heaven, cooking up something demonic for you?" That is the equivalent of my son waking up, walking into the kitchen, rubbing his eyes, and asking his mother, "Mom, could I have eggs and cheese," and my wife turning to him and replying, "Yeah. You can have eggs and cheese. I've been waiting for you to ask for eggs and cheese. I've got two scorpions here under the kitchen sink that I can't wait to give you, Sonny," and she becomes this twisted picture of the wicked witch from the *Wizard of Oz.* "Augh!" Okay, maybe I am taking this a bit far, but the point needs to be made. This is what it looks like in the spiritual realm for you to think suspiciously of God, that as you present your precious heart to Him – a heart that's saved, sanctified, set apart, and with a Father-filter on it– and as you cry out to Him, "Father, please baptize me with Your Holy Spirit," that all of a sudden, oh no, here comes the demon to get you; look out!

Jesus says to not even think that way because if you who are evil in heart know how to give good gifts to your kids, how much more will the Father in heaven give to His kids that ask for the good gift of the Holy Spirit? So please, please, don't make that mistake. Don't throw the baby out with the bath water. Don't look on at spiritual things, like the doctrine of the Baptism of the Holy Spirit, and think, "Well, I don't understand it and, to tell the truth, I'm a little afraid of it, so I am just going to push it away." No, no, no. It is time that you understood it. Remember, Christianity is spiritual because God is Spirit, and those who worship Him must worship Him in spirit and truth.

If you have reached the end of this book, I commend you for having an open enough mind and heart to stay with me through a scriptural exposition of this difficult and divisive doctrine. I want to encourage you with all my heart to consider the claims of the Bible on this essential truth that God has graciously and clearly defined for us in His Word. It is my own personal opinion that the divided heart of the body of Christ on this topic is due mainly to the work of the enemy because he knows the powerful provision of this providential promise. He will go to all lengths to keep you from knowing the power of God's Spirit in your life to be a witness for Jesus to the world around you. Please prayerfully consider what you have read and ask God to show you the truth concerning His will for you in this matter. Although I have attempted to use humor to mitigate some of the more negative connotations of this doctrine, I have also endeavored to keep the focus on Scripture and to allow God to speak His Word to your heart on a matter of utmost importance to Him. I pray that He has been able to accomplish that purpose.

If you would like to receive the Baptism of the Holy Spirit, the following is a sample prayer that you can pray. I would encourage you to add your own words or change words, as the Lord leads you:

Lord, I want all that You have to give me. I realize that I cannot do what You have called me to do in my own strength. I need the power and the boldness I see available through the Baptism of the Holy Spirit. You have promised in Your Word in Luke 11 that You will not withhold this from anyone who asks. In the humility of my humanity, I seek now the provision of Your power. In Jesus' name. Amen.

If you have any further questions regarding this important doctrine, please feel free to contact us at:

Calvary Chapel Fort Lauderdale
2401 West Cypress Creek Road
Fort Lauderdale, Florida 33309
954.977.9673

Please visit us at www.calvaryftl.org